How Does the Sky Seem to Change?

HOUGHTON MIFFLIN HARCOURT

PHOTOGRAPHY CREDITS: (c) © MedioImages/Corbis; 3 (b) ©Ginos Premium Images/Alamy Images; 6 (b) ©photodisc/Getty Images; 7 (t) ©Getty Images; 7 (r) Rubberball/Getty Images; 9 (b) ©CJFAN/Getty Images; 10 (b) Comstock/Getty Images; 11 (b) ©Charles C. Place/Getty Images; 11 (t) ©StockTrek/Photodisc/Getty Images

Printed in Mexico

ISBN: 978-0-544-07224-4

12 13 14 15 0908 21 20 19 18 17

4500665195   A B C D E F G

Be an Active Reader!

 Look at these words.

sun	moon	magnify
star	phases	
shadow	telescope	

 Look for answers to these questions.

What can we see in the daytime sky?

How does the daytime sky seem to change?

What can we see in the nighttime sky?

How does the nighttime sky seem to change?

How can we look at objects in the sky?

What can we see in the daytime sky?

Look up at the sky. Sometimes you can see the sun. The sun is the closest star to Earth. A star is an object in the sky that gives off its own light. The sun gives us light. The sun warms Earth.

Look out the window. Is it sunny today?

sky

sun

clouds

How does the daytime sky seem to change?

Do you see clouds? Sometimes you can see them move. You can watch as their shapes change.

During the day, the sun seems to move across the sky. The sun is not really moving. Earth is! Earth turns every day.

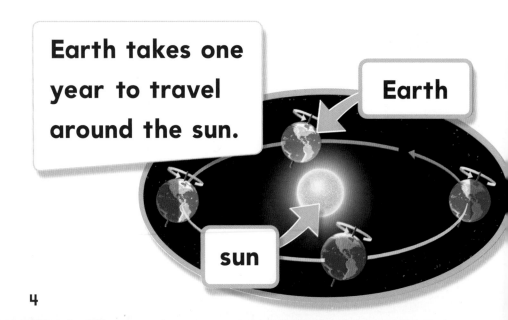

Earth takes one year to travel around the sun.

Earth

sun

Look how the ball's shadow changes throughout the day.

| morning | noon | afternoon |

A shadow is made when an object, such as a tree, blocks the light from the sun. Shadows change as the day goes on. Shadows are long in the morning and afternoon. That is because the sun seems to be at an angle instead of straight overhead. The sun seems to be low in the sky.

What can we see in the nighttime sky?

Is it dark now? If it is, it is probably nighttime. That means the place on Earth where you are standing is facing away from the sun. You can probably see the moon on most nights. The moon is a large sphere of rock.

The moon does not give off its own light.

The sun is a star, too. You just can not see it at night.

Clouds can hide the stars at night.

You can see stars at night, too. Stars are made of gases. They give off their own light.

There are millions of stars in the sky. Stars are very far away. The closer a star is to us, the bigger it will appear.

How does the nighttime sky seem to change?

The moon goes around Earth. Earth moves around the sun. The amount of the moon we can see depends on where Earth and the moon are. The moon does not really change shape.

The different shapes of the moon are called phases.

first quarter   full   third quarter

In each season you can see different stars. That is because of where Earth is as it goes around the sun. You can not see some stars. They are behind the sun. Different stars are hidden at different times of the year.

The sky looks different in each season.

How can we look at objects in the sky?

You can use a telescope to look at objects in the sky. A telescope will magnify objects, or make them look bigger. Small telescopes use lenses. Telescope lenses bend the light. They make objects seem bigger.

telescope

Both telescopes and eyeglasses use lenses.

This photograph was taken through a telescope.

In fact, the person who made the first telescope was an eyeglass maker. That was 400 years ago!

Many telescopes today use both mirrors and lenses.

What would you look at if you could use this telescope?

Use a Magnifier!

Use a hand lens to look at an object. Then take the hand lens away and look at the same thing. What does the hand lens do? Compare your observations with a friend.

 ## Write About the Moon

Which phase of the moon do you like the best? Describe that phase and tell why you like it. Draw a picture to go with your writing.